Wisdom of the Wise

WISDOM OF THE WISE

PITHY AND POINTED SAYINGS
OF THE BEST AUTHORS

SELECTED BY

CAROLINE L. HUNT

OF THE SAN FRANCISCO GIRLS' HIGH SCHOOL

"Words without thoughts are dead sounds; thoughts without words are nothing." — MAX MULLER.

BOSTON
D LOTHROP COMPANY
WASHINGTON STREET OPPOSITE BROMFIELD

INTRODUCTION.

SOLOMON THE WISE said, centuries ago, "Of making many books there is no end;" and a wise man of later times says that no author should add another to the number of books already in the world, unless he can give a good reason for its being. In extenuation of my offense in this respect, I would plead, I did not *make* the book, it *grew*.

For many years a teacher in the Girls' High School, I have been constantly on the alert to find the best way of impressing upon the hearts and minds of my pupils the great principles of right and truth and justice, that lie at the foundation of all good character.

Many plans have been tried, and among them that of placing before the pupils each day a quotation which should contain some truth that

INTRODUCTION.

I desired to impress, some hint in regard to a neglected duty, some gentle reproof for faults committed, or some word of encouragement to new effort.

Selecting for my purpose the noblest thoughts, clothed in the beautiful language of our best authors, I find that the lesson arouses none of the feeling of antagonism that a reproof otherwise administered might occasion; and the responsive glance from a pair of bright eyes has many a time told me of the success of my effort when no word has been spoken. That the seed thus sown bears fruit, I know from letters received from former pupils, who have taken occasion to express their thanks for the benefit they felt they had received.

The plan having come to the knowledge of some of my fellow-teachers, I have frequently been asked to name the book from which I obtained my quotations. This I was unable to do, for the selections had been made from various sources through years of miscellaneous reading, and without a thought of their being used by any one except myself. I was then urged to prepare a volume of the extracts for publication, as such

INTRODUCTION.

a work would be of great value to teachers, and would also prove a welcome gift to the many who best appreciate the shortest sermons.

Being anxious to do the little good I could, I have complied with the request, putting the quotations together in the simplest form, and giving credit to the authors whenever I have been able to do so.

Now, "Armed by faith, and winged by prayer," I send the little volume forth, trusting that it may find a place, and be the means of doing some good in its day and generation.

CAROLINE L. HUNT.

GIRLS' HIGH SCHOOL,
    San Francisco, Cal., July, 1891.

BEAUTY.

'Tis the stainless soul within
That outshines the fairest skin.
SIR A. HUNT.

If eyes were made for seeing,
Then beauty is its own excuse for being.
R. W. EMERSON.

BEING GOOD.

Nothing is to be compared for value with goodness; riches, honor, power, pleasure, learning, the whole world and all in it, are not worth having in comparison with being good.
CHARLES KINGSLEY.

Howe'er it be, it seems to me,
'Tis only noble to be good.
ALFRED TENNYSON.

Be not simply good ; but good for something.
THOREAU.

Goodness and greatness are not means, but ends.
Hath he not always treasures, always friends,
The good great man ?

7

 BOOKS.

Libraries are the wardrobes of literature whence men, properly informed, might bring forth something for ornament, much for curiosity, and more for use. J. DWYER.

Next to acquiring good friends, the best acquisition is that of good books.
C. C. COLTON.

A taste for books is the pleasure and glory of my life. I would not exchange it for the riches of the Indies. GIBBON.

"Dreams, books, are each a world; and books we know,
Are a substantial world, both pure and good;
Round these with tendrils strong as flesh and blood,
Our pastimes and our happiness will grow."
WORDSWORTH.

Books are the food of youth, the delight of old age; the ornament of prosperity, the refuge and comfort of adversity; a delight at home, and no hinderance abroad; a companion by night, in traveling, in the country. CICERO.

8

BRAVERY.

Any coward can fight a battle when he's sure
of winning; but give me the man who has pluck
to fight when he's sure of losing.

GEORGE ELIOT.

Real glory
Springs from the silent conquest of ourselves.

THOMSON.

Wherever a noble deed is done,
   There are the souls of our heroes stirred ;
Wherever a field for truth is won,
   There are our heroes' voices heard.

E. D. PROCTOR.

That courage which arises from the sense of
our duty, and from the fear of offending Him
that made us, acts always in an uniform manner,
and according to the dictates of right reason.

ADDISON.

The brave man is not he who feels no fear,
For that were stupid and irrational ;
But he, whose noble soul its fear subdues,
And bravely dares the danger nature shrinks
     from.   JOANNA BAILLIE.

CHARACTER.

If you would not be known to do anything, never do it.

A man passes for that he is worth.

Character is nature in its highest form.

R. W. EMERSON.

A man cannot speak but he judges himself. With his will or against his will, he draws his portrait to the eye of his companions by every word.

Love, hope, fear, faith — these make humanity; These are its sign, and note, and character.

ROBERT BROWNING.

Conduct is the great profession. Behavior is the perpetual revealing of us. What a man does, tells us what he is.

F. D. HUNTINGTON.

Strong souls
Live like fire-hearted suns, to spend their
strength
In furthest striving action. GEORGE ELIOT.

Character is higher than intellect. A great soul will be strong to live as well as to think.

The American Scholar.

The alms most precious man can give to man
  Are kind and loving words.   Nor come amiss
Warm sympathizing tears to eyes that scan
  The world aright: the only error is
Neglect to do the little good we can.

Charity, taken in its largest extent, is nothing else but the sincere love of God and of our neighbor.   WAKE.

And now abideth faith, hope, charity, these three, but the greatest of these is charity.
                                                   Bible.

The least flower with a brimming cup
May stand and share its dewdrop with another
          near.   E. B. BROWNING.

CONTENTMENT.

He who wants little always has enough.
                                          ZIMMERMAN.

He is richest who is content with the least; for content is the wealth of nature.
                                          SOCRATES.   •

When the best things are not possible, the best may be made of those that are.
                                          HOOKER.

CONTENTMENT.

To secure a contented spirit, measure your desires by your fortunes, and not your fortunes by your desires.   JEREMY TAYLOR.

"Think on your marcies, chile, think on your marcies."

He who isn't contented with what he has wouldn't be contented with what he would like to have.   AUERBACH.

Enjoy your own life without comparing it with that of another.   CONDORCET.

My crown is in my heart, not on my head;
Not decked with diamond and Indian stones,
Nor to be seen : my crown is called content;
A crown it is that seldom kings enjoy.
          SHAKESPEARE.

Sweet are the thoughts that savor of content;
    The quiet mind is richer than a crown;
Sweet are the nights in careless slumber spent;
    The poor estate scorns fortune's angry frown:
Such sweet content, such minds, such sleep, such bliss,
    Beggars enjoy, when princes oft do miss.
          ROBT. GREENE.

12

I've never any pity for conceited people, because I think they carry their comfort about
with them.   GEORGE ELIOT.

Too great confidence in success is the likeli-
est to prevent it; because it hinders us from
making the best use of the advantages which
we enjoy.   ATTERBURY.

Seest thou a man wise in his own conceit?
There is more hope of a fool than of him.

Be not wise in your own conceits.   *Bible.*

Modesty is the politeness of conceit.

CHRISTIANITY.

"Christianity, if it means anything, means
sixteen ounces to the pound, three feet to the
yard, a just weight and just measure.
"It means honesty in all dealings, purity in
all conversation, a charity as broad as the race,
unflinching integrity, sympathy, humanity to
man, loyalty to God. With these there can be
no compromise."

" Politeness is surface Christianity."

13

CONVERSATION.

The first ingredient in conversation is truth, the next good sense, the third, good humor, and the fourth, wit. SIR WM. TEMPLE.

There are three things in speech that ought to be considered before some things are spoken; the manner, the place, and the time.
SOUTHEY.

Words learn'd by rote, a parrot may rehearse,
But talking is not always to converse ;
Not more distinct from harmony divine
The constant creaking of a country sign.
COWPER.

The advantage of conversation is such that, for want of company, a man had better talk to a post than let his thoughts lie smoking and smothering. JEREMY COLLIER.

When you find an antagonist beginning to grow warm, put an end to the dispute by some genteel badinage. CHESTERFIELD.

"If wisdom's ways you wisely seek,
    Five things observe with care ;
Of whom you speak, to whom you speak,
    And how and when and where."

14

"Politeness is to do and say,
The kindest thing in the kindest way."

"Politeness is real kindness, kindly expressed."

No amount of training can make a gentleman or gentlewoman, unless the gentle spirit be within. EMERSON.

In character, in manners, in style, in all things the supreme excellence is simplicity.
LONGFELLOW.

Grace is to the body what good sense is to the mind. ROCHEFOUCAULD.

Love as brethren, be pitiful, be courteous.
Bible.

Good breeding is benevolence in trifles.
LORD CHATHAM.

The person who screams, or uses the superlative degree, or converses with heat, puts whole drawing-rooms to flight. R. W. EMERSON.

Good breeding is the result of much good sense, some good nature, and a little self-denial for the sake of others. CHESTERFIELD.

COURTESY.

"Manners are happy ways of doing things;
each one a stroke of genius or of love, now re-
peated and hardened into usage."

How sweet and gracious even in common
    speech,
Is that fine sense which men call courtesy!
Wholesome as air and genial as the light,
Welcome in every clime as breath of flowers, —
It transmutes aliens into trusting friends,
And gives its owner passport round the globe.
               JAMES T. FIELDS.

"The secret of art in manners may be found
by acting on the principle of making every one
as happy as lies in our power."

    She doeth little kindnesses
    Which most leave undone or despise,
    For naught that sets one's heart at ease
    Or giveth happiness or peace
    Is low-esteeméd in her eyes.
               J. R. LOWELL.

"The true lady never in any way makes her-
self conspicuous, and never does anything un-
necessarily to make other people uncomfortable
or unhappy."

DAUGHTERS.

That our daughters may be as corner-stones
polished after the similitude of a palace.

Bible.

Light-hearted maiden, oh heed thy feet !
 Oh keep where that beam of Paradise falls ;
And only wonder where thou mayst meet
 The blessed ones from its shining walls,
So shalt thou come from the land of dreams
 With love and peace to this world of strife ;
And the life that over that border streams
 Shall be on the path of thy daily life.

W. C. BRYANT.

My daughter, every bond of your life is a
debt ; the right lies in the payment of that
debt ; it can lie nowhere else.

GEORGE ELIOT.

O thou child of many prayers !
Life hath quicksands, Life hath snares !
Care and age come unawares !

Bear through sorrow, wrong, and ruth,
In thy heart the dew of youth ;
On thy lips the smile of truth.

H. W. LONGFELLOW.

DEATH.

Death loves a shining mark, a signal blow.

SHAKESPEARE.

Green be the turf above thee,
   Friend of my better days ;
None knew thee but to love thee,
   Nor named thee but to praise.

FITZ-GREENE HALLECK.

He was a man take him for all in all ;
We shall not look upon his like again.

SHAKESPEARE.

Death is the dropping of the flower that the fruit may swell.

H. W. BEECHER.

" 'Tis the cessation of our breath.
Silent and motionless we lie ;
And no one knoweth more than this."

Leaves have their time to fall ;
   And flowers to wither at the north wind's
      breath;
And stars to set, — but all —
   Thou hast all seasons for thine own, O Death!

MRS. HEMANS.

" E'en such is man; who lives by breath,
Is here, now there, in life and death."

There is no Death! what seems so is transition;
  This life of mortal breath
Is but a suburb of the life elysian,
  Whose portal we call Death.
                    H. W. LONGFELLOW.

  " The living are the only dead;
    The dead live — nevermore to die ;
  And often, when we mourn them fled;
    They never were so nigh ! "

Death is delightful.   Death is dawn,
The waking from a weary night
Of fevers unto truth and light.
                    JOAQUIN MILLER.

DILIGENCE.

  "Diligence is the philosopher's stone that
turns everything into gold."

    " All good of earth, e'en Heaven itself
    By diligence is won."

See'st thou a man diligent in his business?
he shall stand before kings.

  Diligent in business, fervent in spirit, serving
the Lord.   *Bible.*

DOING GOOD.

Neglect no opportunity of doing good, nor check thy desire of doing it, by a vain fear of what may happen.   ATTERBURY.

Count that day lost whose low-descending sun,
Views from thy hand, no worthy action done.
                                        ADRIAN.

Doing good is the only certainly happy action of a man's life.   SIR PHILIP SIDNEY.

What do we live for if not to make life less difficult to each other.   GEORGE ELIOT.

We can do more good by being good than in any other way.   ROWLAND HILL.

Learn the luxury of doing good.
                                        GOLDSMITH.

He who receives a good turn should never forget it; he who does one should never remember it.   CHARSON.

Oh! whatever the fortune a man may have won,
A kindness depends on the way it is done;
And though poor be our purse, and though narrow our span,
Let us all try to do a good turn when we can.
                                        CHARLES SWAIN.

DOING GOOD.

Do all the good you can and don't make a
fuss about it.   CHARLES DICKENS.

" Do good, shun evil, live not thou
    As if at death thy being died ;
Nor error's siren voice allow
    To draw thy steps from truth aside."

You will do good, less by what you say or do
or even give, than by what you are.
                                    DR. PEABODY.

No opportunities for gaining or doing good
ever fall in our way, that will not if improved,
make our lives richer and happier.

No opportunities of good are ever lost, through
our neglect, without being, some day, missed
and regretted.   M. H. HOWELL.

Be good, sweet maid, and let who will be clever,
    Do noble things, not dream them all day long :
And so make life, death, and that vast forever
            One grand sweet song.
                            CHARLES KINGSLEY.

DUTY.

Great powers and natural gifts do not bring privileges to their possessor so much as they bring duties. H. W. BEECHER.

There is not a moment without some duty.
CICERO.

What it is our duty to do we must do because it is right, not because any one can demand it of us. WHEWELL.

" With all thy heart love God above,
And, as thyself, thy neighbor love."

" Every noble life is a life of duty, and that duty is synonymous with labor."

Be sure that God
Ne'er dooms to waste the strength he deigns
impart. ROBERT BROWNING.

He who is false to present duty breaks a thread in the loom, and will find a flaw, when he may have forgotten its cause.
H. W. BEECHER.

" Every hour that fleets so slowly,
Has its task to do or bear;
Luminous the crown and holy,
If thou set each gem with care."

DUTY.

Resolved, never to do anything, which, if I should see in another, I should count a just occasion to despise him for, or to think any way more meanly of him. JONATHAN EDWARDS.

God gives all his creatures some duty each day,
And mine is, perhaps, just to trust and obey.
MARGARET E. SANGSTER.

God never imposes a duty without giving the time to do it. RUSKIN.

"Little duties are golden pins to fasten the mantle of God's love securely about us."

Build to-day, then, strong and sure,
 With a firm and ample base,
And ascending and secure
 Shall to-morrow find its place.
H. W. LONGFELLOW.

There is nothing in the universe that I fear but that I shall not know all my duty or shall fail to do it. MARY LYON.

"Your duty for to-day does not lie in a foreign land."

23

" He who buys what he does not need will often need what he cannot buy."

Never buy what you do not want because it is cheap.   FRANKLIN.

Run never in debt, but pay as you go;
A man free from debt feels a heaven below;
It needs a great effort the spirit to brace
'Gainst the terror that dwells in a creditor's
         face.   B. P. SHILLABER.

Beware of little expenses; a small leak will sink a great ship.   B. FRANKLIN.

Economy is the parent of integrity, of liberty, and of ease.   DR. JOHNSON.

EDUCATION.

Learning by study must be won;
'Twas ne'er entailed from son to son.
                                              GAY.

Those who trust us educate us.
                                       GEORGE ELIOT.

Without education men are like bears and wolves.   LUTHER.

Education begins the gentleman; but reading, good company, and reflection must finish him.
                                             LOCKE.

24

EDUCATION.

Every man who rises above the common level receives two educations: the first from his instructors; the second, the most personal and important, from himself.   GIBBON.

"A good education consists in a combination of good habits."

Perhaps the most valuable result of all education is the ability to make yourself do the thing you have to do, when it ought to be done, whether you like it or not; it is the first lesson that ought to be learned, and however early a man's training begins, it is probably the last lesson that he learns thoroughly.

T. H. HUXLEY.

The true aim of the highest education is to give character, rather than knowledge, to train men to be, rather than to know.

MARK HOPKINS.

The first thing in education is to encourage a habit of observation and inquiry. When your child asks, "What is the use of this?" "Why is that?" don't call it troublesome. The best education is that which is the answer to our own inquiries.   ROBERTSON.

ENEMIES — FAITH.

It's poor foolishness to run down your enemies.
GEORGE ELIOT.

'Tis death to me to be at enmity; I hate it, and desire all good men's love. SHAKESPEARE.

FAITH.

I know not where those islands lift
   Their fronded palms in air,
I only know they cannot drift
   Beyond God's love and care.
J. G. WHITTIER.

Faith is the subtle chain
That binds us to the Infinite: the voice
Of a deep life within.
ELIZABETH OAKES SMITH.

There is a day of sunny rest
   For every dark and troubled night,
And grief may bide an evening guest,
   But joy shall come with early light.

The light of smiles shall fill again
   The lids that overflow with tears,
And weary hours of woe and pain
   Are promises of happier years.
W. C. BRYANT.

26

FALSEHOOD.

Sin has many tools, but a lie is the handle
that fits them all. O. W. HOLMES.

A lie has no legs, and cannot stand; but it
has wings and can fly far and wide.
BISHOP WARBURTON.

Liars are the cause of all the sins and crimes
in the world. EPICTETUS.

Dare to be true. Nothing can need a lie;
A fault which needs it most, grows two thereby.
HERBERT.

Lying lips are abomination to the Lord; but
they that deal truly are his delight. *Bible.*

Oh! what a tangled web we weave
When first we practice to deceive.
SCOTT.

He who tells a lie is not sensible how great a
task he undertakes, for he must be forced to
invent twenty more to maintain one. POPE.

And he that does one fault at first,
And lies to hide it, makes it two.
WATTS.

A lie is like a vizard, that may cover the face
indeed but can never become it. SOUTH.

Be firm; one constant element in luck
Is genuine solid old Teutonic pluck;
See yon tall shaft; it felt the earthquake's thrill,
Clung to its base, and greets the sunrise still.

O. W. HOLMES.

Be firm of heart;
" By fusion of unnumbered years
A continent its vastness rears!
A drop, 'tis said, through flint will wear;
Toil on, and nature's conquest share !
Toil on ! "

FORGIVENESS.

" I can forgive, but I cannot forget," is only
another way of saying, I will not forgive. A
forgiveness ought to be like a cancelled note,
torn in two and burned up, so that it never can
be shown against the man.

H. W. BEECHER.

He that cannot forgive others breaks the
bridge over which he must pass himself; for
every man has need to be forgiven.

LORD HERBERT OF CHERBURY.

Humanity is never so beautiful as when praying for forgiveness, or else forgiving another.

RICHTER.

No man is free who cannot command himself.
EPICTETUS.

True liberty can exist only when justice is equally administered.   LORD MANSFIELD.

Liberty and Union, now and forever, one and inseparable.   DANIEL WEBSTER.

Lord of the Universe! shield us and guide us,
   Trusting Thee always, through shadow and
      sun!
Thou hast united us, who shall divide us?
   Keep us, O keep us — the Many in one.
O. W. HOLMES.

FRIENDSHIP.

"A false friend, like a shadow, attends only while the sun shines."

"The noblest part of a friend is an honest boldness in the notifying of errors. He that tells me of a fault aiming at my good, I must think him wise and faithful; wise in spying that which I see not; faithful in a plain admonition, not tainted with flattery."   FELTHAM.

" Be true to your word, your work and your friend."

29

"Prevent a friend from doing you good, impress him with the idea that he is of no use to you, and his affection will cool. But ask a man for little services he is ready to render, let him know and keep in his mind that he has conferred a benefit upon you, and he will like you all the more for it, become interested in your welfare, and feel real devotion for you. I have never known this experiment to fail."

We should praise our friends — our near and dear ones — we should look on and think of their virtues till their faults fade away.

H. B. STOWE.

Friendship is a strong and habitual inclination in two persons to promote the good and happiness of each other. ADDISON.

'Tis thus that on the choice of friends,
Our good or evil name depends. GAY.

Inquiries from friends fret and gall more, and the memory of them is not so easily obliterated.

ARBUTHNOT.

It is a rare friendship that will tell a man his faults.

HENRY WARD BEECHER.

30

FRIENDSHIP.

Friendship improves happiness, and abates misery, by the doubling of our joy and the dividing of our grief.   Cicero.

The firmest friendships have been formed in mutual adversity; as iron is most strongly united by the fiercest flame.   Colton.

Friendship is the shadow of the evening, which strengthens with the setting sun of life.
    La Fontaine.

A long novitiate of acquaintance should precede the vows of friendship.
    Lord Bolingbroke.

"A friend is most a friend of whom the best remains to learn."

"True friends visit us in prosperity only when invited, but in adversity they come uninvited."

"That friendship only is indeed genuine when two friends, without speaking a word to each other, can nevertheless find happiness in being together."

Better be a nettle in the side of your friend than his echo.   R. W. Emerson.

31

"True friendship's laws are by this law expressed:
Welcome the coming, speed the parting guest."

HOMER.

The only reward of virtue is virtue; the only way to have a friend is to be one.

R. W. EMERSON.

It is the ordinary lot of people to have no friends, if they themselves care for nobody.

THACKERAY.

GIVING.

One must be poor to know the luxury of giving!

GEORGE ELIOT.

A word warm from the heart enriches me.

Flowers and fruits are always fit presents; flowers because they are a proud assertion that a ray of beauty outvalues all the utilities of the world. Fruits are acceptable gifts, because they are the flower of commodities, and admit of fantastic values being attached to them.

R. W. EMERSON.

Who gives himself with his alms feeds three;
Himself, his hungering neighbor and me.

J. R. LOWELL.

32

St. Augustine described the nature of God as a circle whose center was everywhere, and its circumference nowhere.

God is a spirit, and they that worship him must worship him in spirit and in truth.

Bible.

All are but parts of one stupendous whole,
Whose body Nature is, and God the soul.

Pope.

God is a spirit, infinite, eternal and unchangeable, in his being, wisdom, power, holiness, justice, goodness and truth.   *Catechism.*

GOD'S LOVE.

" Could we with ink the ocean fill,
    Were the whole earth of parchment made,
Were every blade of grass a quill,
    And every man a scribe by trade,
To write the love of God above
    Would drain the ocean dry,
Nor could the scroll contain the whole
    Though stretched from sky to sky."

There is no creature so small and abject, that it representeth not the goodness of God.

Thomas À Kempis.

GOD'S LOVE.

God is love, His mercy brightens
 All the path in which we rove;
Bliss He wakes, and woe he lightens,
 God is wisdom, God is love.

JOHN BOWRING.

There's nothing bright above, below,
From flowers that bloom to stars that glow,
But in its light my soul can see
Some feature of Thy Deity.

THOMAS MOORE.

Love, and God will pay you with the capacity
of more love; for love is Heaven — love is God
within you.

ROBERTSON.

Henceforth my heart shall sigh no more
For olden time and holier shore ;
God's love and blessing, then and there,
Are now and here and everywhere.

J. G. WHITTIER.

God's fullness flows around our incompleteness;
Round our restlessness, his rest.

E. B. BROWNING.

The superfluous blossoms on a fruit tree are
meant to symbolize the large way in which God
loves to do pleasant things.

H. W. BEECHER.

I've heard of hearts unkind, kind deeds
With coldness still returning ;
Alas, the gratitude of men
Hath often left me mourning.

WORDSWORTH.

The gratitude of most men is but a secret desire of receiving greater benefits.

ROCHRFOUCAULD.

"Thankfulness is the beginning of gratitude ; gratitude is the completion of thankfulness."
He that hath nature in him, must be grateful ;
'Tis the Creator's primary great law
That links the chain of beings to each other.

MADDEN.

A grateful mind
By owing owes not, but still pays, at once
Indebted and discharged.

MILTON.

HAPPINESS.

I count myself in nothing else so happy
As in a soul remembering my good friends.

I would that happiness were gold, that I
Might cast my largess of it to the crowd.

SHAKESPEARE.

To persevere in any evil course makes you unhappy in this life.　　　　　WAKE.

" A happy temper like the Æolian harp, sings to every breeze."

Happy are they, my son, who shall learn from thy example not to despair; but shall remember, that though the day is past, and their strength is wasted, there yet remains one effort to be made; that reformation is never hopeless, nor sincere endeavor ever unassisted.

　　　　　　　　　　SAMUEL JOHNSON.

All who joy would win must share it —
Happiness was born a twin.　　　BYRON.

Our happiness in this world depends on the affection we are enabled to inspire.

　　　　　　　　　　DUCHESS DU PLASTIN.

He is happy whose circumstances suit his temper, but he is more excellent who can suit his temper to any circumstances.　　HUME.

Make people happy, and there will not be half the quarreling or a tenth part of the wickedness there is.　　　　LYDIA M. CHILD.

HEAVEN.

Go wing thy flight from star to star,
From world to luminous world, as far
As the universe spreads its flaming walls;
Take all the pleasures of all the spheres
And multiply each through endless years,
One minute of heaven is worth them all.

THOMAS MOORE.

Think of heaven with hearty purposes and peremptory designs to get thither.

JEREMY TAYLOR.

The Power that call'd thee into life has skill to
    make thee live,
A place of refuge can provide, another being
    give;
Can clothe thy perishable form with beauty rich
    and rare,
And, "when He takes his jewels up," grant thee
    a station there.   BISHOP RICHARD MANT.

A soul inspired with the warmest aspirations after celestial beatitude keeps its powers attentive.

DR. I. WATTS.

" For love is heaven, and heaven is love."

History is the complement of Poetry.
SIR J. STEVENS.

History is a mighty drama, enacted upon the theater of time, with suns for lamps, and Eternity for a background. CARLYLE.

All literature writes the character of the wise man.

"What is history," said Napoleon, "but a fable agreed upon?"

The Doric temple preserves the semblance of the wooden cabin in which the Dorian dwelt. The Chinese pagoda is plainly a Tartar tent.
R. W. EMERSON.

HOME.

Home's not merely four square walls,
  Though with pictures hung and gilded;
Home is where Affection calls, —
  Filled with shrines the heart hath builded!
Home! go watch the faithful dove,
  Sailing 'neath the heaven above us;
Home is where there's one to love!
  Home is where there's one to love us!
CHARLES SWAIN.

HOME.

The ornaments of a home are the friends who frequent it.   EMERSON.

The strength of a nation, especially of a republican nation, is in the intelligent and well-ordered homes of the people.
MRS. SIGOURNEY.

Home is the resort
Of love, of joy, of peace and plenty, where
Supported and supporting, polished friends
And dear relations mingle into bliss.
THOMPSON.

By the fireside still the light is shining,
The children's arms round the parents twining.
From love so sweet, O who would roam?
Be it ever so homely, home is home.
D. M. MULOCK.

Home is the sacred refuge of our life.
DRYDEN.

" Home, ye may be high or lowly,
Hearts alone can make you holy.
Be the dwelling e'er so small,
Having love it boasteth all."

The sweetest words ear ever heard are mother, home, and heaven.

HONESTY.

Honesty coupled to beauty is to have honey
a sauce to sugar.   SHAKESPEARE.

An honest death is better than a dishonest
life.   SOCRATES.

What is becoming is honest, and whatever is
honest must always be becoming.   CICERO.

Heaven that made me honest, made me more
Than ever king did when he made a lord.
                               ROWE.

The more honesty a man has, the less he
affects the air of a saint.   LAVATER.

There is no sound basis of power but honesty.
                           J. G. HOLLAND.

Ay, sir ; to be honest, as this world goes, is to
be one man pick'd out of two thousand.
                               SHAKESPEARE.

An honest man is the noblest work of God.
                               POPE.

Lands mortgaged may return and more es-
      teemed ;
But honesty once pawned is ne'er redeemed.
                               MIDDLETON.

An idle youth — a needy age.

Idleness is the mother of all mischief.

Old Proverb.

An idle brain is the Devil's work-shop.

Absence of occupation is not rest,
A mind quite vacant is a mind distressed.

COWPER.

An idler is a watch that wants both hands;
As useless if it goes as if it stands.

COWPER.

If you have but an hour, will you not improve that hour, instead of idling it away?

CHESTERFIELD.

INDOLENCE.

Lives spent in indolence, and therefore sad.

COWPER.

Who conquers indolence will conquer all the rest.   ZIMMERMAN.

I look upon indolence as a sort of suicide; for the man is effectually destroyed, though the appetite of the brute may survive.

LORD CHESTERFIELD.

INDUSTRY.

Industry hath annexed thereto the finest fruits and the richest rewards.   BARROW.

Round swings the hammer of industry,
    Quickly the sharp chisel rings,
And the heart of the toiler has throbbings
    That stir not the bosom of kings, —
He the true ruler and conqueror,
    He the true king of his race,
Who nerveth his arm for life's combat,
    And looks the whole world in the face.
                            DR. F. MCCARTHY.

In every rank, or great or small
'Tis industry supports us all.   GAY.

Never the ocean wave falters in flowing;
Never the little seed stops in its growing;
More and more richly the rose heart keeps
        glowing,
Till from the nourishing stem it is riven.
                            F. S. OSGOOD.

A man who gives his children habits of industry, provides for them better than by giving them a fortune.   WHATELY.

42

INFLUENCE.

If we work upon marble, it will perish; if we
work upon brass, time will efface it; if we rear
temples, they will crumble into dust; but if we
work upon immortal minds, if we imbue them
with right principles, with the just fear of God
and love of our fellowmen, we engrave on those
tablets something which will brighten to all
eternity.   DANIEL WEBSTER.

Our many deeds, the thoughts that we have
        thought,
They go out from us thronging every hour;
And in them each is folded up a power
That on the earth doth move them to and
        fro;
And mighty are the marvels they have wrought
In hearts we know not and may never know.

"There is no end to the sky,
  And the stars are everywhere,
  And time is eternity,
  And the here is over there;
  For the common deeds of the common day
  Are ringing bells in the far away."

INFLUENCE.

Life is made up, not of great sacrifices or duties, but of little things, in which smiles, and kindnesses and small obligations given habitually, are what win and preserve the heart and secure comfort.   SIR H. DAVY.

Air and manner are more expressive than words.   S. RICHARDSON.

You cannot afford to do anything but what is good. You are on dress parade all the time.
                    BOB BURDETTE.

A man's strength in this life is often greater from some single word, remembered and cherished, than in arms or armor.
                    H. W. BEECHER.

No action, whether foul or fair,
Is ever done, but it leaves somewhere
A record written by fingers ghostly,
As a blessing or a curse; but mostly,
In the greater weakness or greater strength
Of the acts which follow it, till at length,
The wrongs of ages are redressed,
And the justice of God made manifest.
                    H. W. LONGFELLOW.

44

INFLUENCE.

As ships meet at sea, a moment together when words of greeting must be spoken, and then away upon the deep, so men meet in this world; and I think we should cross no man's path without hailing him, and, if he needs, giving him supplies.   H. W. BEECHER.

Every man however humble his station, or feeble his power, exercises some influence on those who are about him, for good or for evil.
                                        A. SEDGWICK.

"The seed we sow within the soil to-day,
   The morrow's sun will ripen into grain:
The deeds we do within this mortal clay
   Are steps by which the summit we may gain
            To-morrow."
      Our echoes roll from soul to soul,
      And grow forever and forever.
                                        TENNYSON.

Cast forth thy act, thy word, into the ever-lasting, ever-working universe: it is a seed grain that cannot die: unnoticed to-day, it will be found flourishing as a banyan grove, perhaps, alas, as a hemlock forest, after a thousand years.   CARLYLE.

45

INFLUENCE.

O'er wayward childhood wouldst thou hold firm
    rule,
And sun thee in the light of happy faces;
Love, Hope and Patience, these must be thy
    graces,
And in thine own heart let them first keep
    school.   COLERIDGE.

    Sow love and taste its fruitage pure,
      Sow peace and reap its harvest bright,
    Sow sunshine on the rock and moor,
      And find a harvest-home of light.
                  HORATIUS BONAR.

Not one sentence that passes these lips of
ours but must be an invisibly prolonged influence, not dying away into silence, but living
away into the words and deeds of others.
                F. R. HAVERGAL.

" The influence of woman more or less affects,
for good or for evil, the entire destinies of
mankind."

" Though the head may rule, it is the heart
that influences."

The home may be regarded as the most influential school of civilization. The mother, far more than the father, influences the action and conduct of the child, for her good example is of much greater importance in the house.

SAMUEL SMILES.

Nor is a true soul ever born for naught,
   Wherever any such hath lived and died,
There hath been something, fortune, freedom, wrought,
   Some bulwark leveled on the evil side.

J. R. LOWELL.

INGRATITUDE.

I hate ingratitude in a man, more
Than lying, vainness, babbling, drunkenness,
Or any taint of vice.   SHAKESPEARE.

He that is ungrateful has no guilt but one ; all other crimes may pass for virtues in him.

DR. YOUNG.

" Ingratitude is the Aaron's rod which swallows up and comprises in itself all the lesser vices."

47

JUSTICE.

Justice while she winks at crimes
Stumbles on innocence sometimes.
BUTLER.

Just men are only free, the rest are slaves.
CHAPMAN.

Man is unjust, but God is just; and finally
justice triumphs.   LONGFELLOW.

What stronger breastplate than a heart untainted,
Thrice is he armed who hath his quarrel just,
And he but naked, though locked up in steel,
Whose conscience with injustice is corrupted.
SHAKESPEARE.

"Justice is the foundation, or mainstay of
kingdoms, the rock on which kingdoms are
founded."

"Faith, fidelity, truth, honesty, is the ground-
work of Justice."

"Justice consists in doing no injury to men:
decency, in giving them no offense."

"Unsullied faith, of soul sincere,
Of justice pure the sister fair."

" To think kindly one of another is good, to speak kindly one of another is better, and to act kindly one to another is best of all."

> " How many acts of kindness
>   A little child may do,
> Although it has so little strength
>   And little wisdom, too!
> It wants a loving spirit
>   Much more than strength, to prove
> How many things a child may do
>   For others, by its love."

KNOWLEDGE.

Knowledge is that which next to virtue, truly and essentially raises one man above another.

ADDISON.

He that doth not know those things which are of use for him to know is but an ignorant man, whatever he may know besides.

There is a knowledge which is very proper to man, and lies level to human understanding — the knowledge of our Creator and of the duty we owe to him.   TILLOTSON.

KNOWLEDGE.

Knowledge is a rude, unprofitable mass
The mere material with which Wisdom builds,
Till smoothed and squared and fitted to its
      place,
Does but encumber what it seems to enrich.
Knowledge is proud that he has learned so
      much ;
Wisdom is humble that he knows no more.

COWPER.

What we acquire is knowledge; what we develop is culture.   J. G. HOLLAND.

The Lord is God of knowledge, and by him actions are weighed.   *Bible.*

The desire of knowledge, like the thirst for riches, increases ever with the acquisition of it.   STERNE.

One never knows that he knows anything till he finds himself able to tell others of it.

BRAINERD KELLOGG.

Knowledge and wisdom far from being one,
Have oft times no connection.

                   Knowledge dwells
In heads replete with thoughts of other men ;
Wisdom in minds attentive to their own.

COWPER.

"Strict laws are like steel bodice, good for
    growing limbs ;
But when the joints are knit, they are not helps
    but burdens."

We must not make a scarecrow of the law,
Setting it up to fear the birds of prey,
And let it keep one shape till custom make it
Their perch and not their terror. SHAKESPEARE.

All law that man is obliged by, is reducible to
the law of nature, the positive law of God in his
word, and the law of man enacted by the civil
power.   SOUTH.

Law is the science in which the greatest
powers of the understanding are applied to the
greatest number of facts.   DR. JOHNSON.

LESSONS.

One of the lessons a woman most rarely learns,
is never to talk to an angry or a drunken man.
                          GEORGE ELIOT.

Let our lives be pure as snow-fields, where
our footsteps leave a mark, but not a stain.
                    MADAME SWETCHINE.

We sleep, but the loom of life never stops; and the pattern which was weaving when the sun went down is weaving when it comes up to-morrow.

God asks no man whether he will accept life. That is not the choice. You *must* take it. The only choice is *how*. H. W. BEECHER.

Life is a short day; but it is a working day. Activity may lead to evil; but inactivity cannot be led to good. HANNAH MORE.

"Life is a sum, and it becomes us to do it properly as it can be done but once."

> It seems that life is all a void,
> On selfish thoughts alone employed;
> That length of days is not a good,
> Unless their use be understood.
> JANE TAYLOR.

Life alone can impart life, and though we should burst, we can only be valued as we make ourselves valuable. R. W. EMERSON.

> Not what we would, but what we must,
> Make up the sum of living.
> R. H. STODDARD.

LIFE.

Life like a dome of many colored glass,
Stains the white radiance of eternity.
SHELLEY.

My life is the living force I exert among
men. STEWART.

We live in deeds, not years; in thoughts, not
    breaths;
In feelings, not in figures on a dial.
We should count time by heart throbs.
He most lives,
Who thinks most, feels the noblest, acts the
    best. P. J. BAILEY.

Every man's life is within the present; for
the past is spent and done with, and the future
is uncertain. ANTONINUS.

Circles are prais'd not that abound
In largeness, but th' exactly round:
So life we praise, that does excel
Not in much time, but acting well.
WALLER.

The golden moments in the stream of life
rush past us, and we see nothing but sand; the
angels come to visit us, and we only know them
when they are gone. GEORGE ELIOT.

53

He that loveth not, knoweth not God; for God is love.

Let brotherly love continue. *Bible.*

Love is ownership. We own whom we love. The universe is God's because he loves.
H. W. BEECHER.

We can make it a Christian duty, not only to love, but to be loving — not only to be true friends, but to show ourselves friendly.
H. B. STOWE.

With all thy heart love God above,
And as thyself thy neighbor love.

MAN.

Make yourself an honest man, and then you may be sure that there is one rascal less in the world. CARLYLE.

Men are frequently like tea, their real strength and goodness is not drawn out till they have been for a short time in hot water.
Cruikshank's Almanac.

Young men think old men fools, and old men know young men to be so. *Ray's Proverbs.*

MAN.

"Man — a big animal who treads on things, roars subdued thunder when dinner isn't ready, and feeds himself like an ox."

The real man is one who always finds excuses for others, but never excuses himself.

H. W. BEECHER.

Men of public spirit differ rather in their circumstances than their virtues; and the man who does all he can in a low station, is more a hero than he who omits any worthy action he is able to accomplish in a great one.

SIR R. STEELE.

What tho' on hamely fare we dine,
　Wear hoddin gray, and a' that?
Gie fools their silks and knaves their wine,
　A man's a man for a' that.

BURNS.

How wonderful a being is man, when viewed in the light of his achievements.

J. G. HOLLAND.

Man is God's creation. Everything else is the nursery and nurse of man.

H. W. BEECHER.

"Immodest words admit of no defense,
For want of modesty is want of sense."

" Modesty is the peculiar characteristic of a virtuous woman, and is the safeguard of all virtue."

Modesty is to Merit as Shades to Figures in a Picture, giving it Strength and Beauty.

LA BRUYÈRE.

Mere Bashfulness without Merit is awkward ; and Merit without Modesty insolent. But Modest Merit has a double claim to acceptance.

HUGHES.

MOTHERS.

The child taketh the most of his nature from the mother, besides speech, manners, and inclination, which are agreeable to the conditions of their mothers.   EDMUND SPENSER.

Even He that died for us upon the cross, in the last hour, in the unutterable agony of death was mindful of his mother, as if to teach us that this holy love should be our last worldly thought, the last point of earth from which the soul should take its flight to Heaven.

H. W. LONGFELLOW.

MOTHERS.

My mother's voice ! how often creep
   Its accents o'er my lonely hours ;
Like healing sent on wings of sleep,
   Or dew to the unconscious flowers.
I can forget her melting prayer
   When leaping pulses madly fly,
But on the chill, unbroken air
   Her gentle tones come stealing by,
And years and sin and manhood flee,
   And leave me at my mother's knee.
N. P. WILLIS.

A mother's example sinks down into the heart of her child, like snow-flakes into the heart of the ocean.   H. O. WARD.

On every land — in every clime —
   True to her sacred cause,
Filled by that effluence sublime
   From which her strength she draws,
Still is the mother's heart the same —
   The mother's lot as tried :
Then, Oh ! may Nations guard that name
   With filial power and pride.
CHARLES SWAIN.

The mother's heart is the child's school-room.
H. W. BEECHER.

Men's muscles move better when their souls are making merry music.   GEORGE ELIOT.

There's music in the sighing of a reed:
There's music in the gushing of a rill:
There's music in all things if men had ears:
Their earth is but an echo of the spheres.

BYRON.

— Feeling hearts — touch them but rightly —
    pour
A thousand melodies unheard before.

MOORE.

All one's life is music, if one touches the notes rightly, and in time.   RUSKIN.

NEATNESS.

Certainly this is a duty, not a sin,
Cleanliness is next to godliness.

JOHN WESLEY.

Cleanliness was ever esteemed to proceed from a due reverence to God.   BACON.

"True gentility shows itself in a neat, well-ordered home, where sunshine and joy abound, and where all the inmates are linked together by the golden chains of love."

58

"If you intend to do a mean thing, wait till to-morrow. If you are to do a noble thing, do it now."

"As one lamp lights another, nor grows less,
So nobleness enkindleth nobleness."

OBEDIENCE.

Obedience is a complicated act of virtue, and many graces are exercised in one act of obedience. JEREMY TAYLOR.

To prayer, repentance and obedience due,
Though but endeavored with sincere intent;
Mine ear shall not be slow, mine eye not shut.
MILTON.

"Government must compel the obedience of individuals; otherwise who will seek its protection or fear its vengeance."

Sons of heav'n and earth,
Attend: That thou art happy, owe to God:
That thou continuest such, owe to thyself,
That is to thy obedience: therein stand.
MILTON.

Obey them that have the rule over you, and submit yourselves. *Bible.*

59

" Nothing helps the memory so much as order and classification."

Order is Heaven's first law and this confessed,
Some are and must be greater than the rest.

POPE.

Science in all its discoveries, tends to the discovery of universal order.   FLEMING.

Order is the sanity of the mind, the health of the body, the peace of the city, the security of the State.   SOUTHEY.

PEACE.

Speak gently ! He who gave his life
    To bend man's stubborn will
When elements were fierce with strife
    Said to them, Peace, be still.

BATES.

Peace, greatness best becomes.
Calm pow'r doth guide,
With a far more imperious stateliness,
Than all the swords of violence can do :
And easier gains those ends she tends unto.

DANIEL.

PATIENCE.

"If thou bearest slight provocations with patience, it shall be imputed unto thee for wisdom, and if thou wipest them from thy remembrance, thy heart shall feel rest, thy mind shall not reproach thee."

If you've tried and have not won,
    Never stop for crying;
All that's good and great is done
    Just by patient trying.
                            PHŒBE CARY.

It is easy finding reasons why other people should be patient.   GEORGE ELIOT.

Practice patience, I can tell you that requires nearly as much practice as music; and we are continually losing our lesson when the master comes.   JOHN RUSKIN.

I worked with patience, which is almost power.
                            E. B. BROWNING.

That thou mayst pray for them thy foes are
        given:
I bring thee fretful friends that thou mayst
        train
Thy soul to patience.   KEBLE.

"Never give up; for the wisest is boldest,
Knowing that Providence mingles the cup,
And of all maxims, the best as the oldest,
Is the true watchword of ' Never give up.' "

" He conquers who endures."

Attempt the end and never stand to doubt:
Nothing's so hard but search will find it out.

HERRICK.

Those who attain any excellence commonly
spend life in one common pursuit; for excellence
is not often gained upon easier terms.

DR. S. JOHNSON.

Attempt the end, and never stand to doubt!
Nothing's so hard but search will find it out.

R. HERRICK.

PATRIOTISM.

I fancy the proper means of increasing the
love we bear our native country is to reside
some time in a foreign one.   SHENSTONE.

Breathes there the man with soul so dead
Who never to himself hath said,
   " This is my own, my native land ? "

SCOTT.

PATRIOTISM.

Be just and fear not.
Let all the ends thou aim'st at be thy country's,
Thy God's and truth's: then if thou fallest, O
     Cromwell!
Thou fallest a blessed martyr.
SHAKESPEARE.

Strike — till the last armed foe expires;
Strike — for your altars and your fires;
Strike — for the green graves of your sires,
God and your native land!
FITZ-GREENE HALLECK.

One flag, one land, one heart, one hand,
One nation evermore.   HOLMES.

O Land of lands! to thee we give
    Our prayers, our hopes, our service free,
For thee thy sons shall nobly live,
    And at thy need shall die for thee!
J. G. WHITTIER.

Our Country first, their glory and their pride,
Land of their hopes, land where their fathers
    died,
When in the right, they'll keep thy honor bright,
When in the wrong, they'll die to set it right.
JAMES T. FIELDS.

PRAYER.

When you lie down, close your eyes with a
short prayer, commit yourself into the hands of
your faithful Creator ; and when you have done
trust Him with yourself; as you must do when
you are dying.   JEREMY TAYLOR.

Be not afraid to pray — to pray is right ;
Pray if thou canst in hope, — O, ever pray,
If hope be weak and sick with long delay
Pray in the darkness, if thou hast no light.
                            HARTLEY COLERIDGE.

Let prayer be the key of the morning, and the
bolt of the evening.   MATTHEW HENRY.

Let the day have a blessed baptism by giving
your first waking thoughts into the bosom of
God. The first hour of the morning is the
rudder of the day.   H. W. BEECHER.

Sister, the holy maid does well
Who counts her beads in convent cell,
    Where pale devotion lingers ;
But she who serves the sufferer's needs,
Whose prayers are spent in loving deeds,
May trust the Lord will count her beads,
    As well as human fingers.
                            O. W. HOLMES.

64

PRAYER.

I pray the prayer of Plato old,
   God make thee beautiful within,
And let thine eyes the good behold,
   In everything save sin.
J. G. Whittier.

Prayer is Innocence's friend, and willingly flieth
    incessant,
'Twixt the earth and the sky, the carrier pigeon
    of Heaven.   H. W. Longfellow.

Though oft like letters traced in sand
   My weak resolves have passed away,
In mercy lend thy helping hand
   Unto my prayers to-day.
J. G. Whittier.

Thrice blest whose lives are faithful prayers,
   Whose loves in higher love endure,
   Whose souls possess themselves so pure,
Or is there blessedness like theirs ?
Tennyson.

The blue sky is the temple's arch,
   Its transept earth and air,
The music of its starry march
   The chorus of its prayer.
J. G. Whittier.

PRAYER.

It is not well for a man to pray cream and live skim milk.   H. W. BEECHER.

More things are wrought by prayer than this world dreams of.   TENNYSON.

Trouble and perplexity drive us to prayer, and prayer drives away perplexity and trouble.
    MELANCTHON.

Sinning makes you leave off praying, and praying makes you leave off sinning.
    J. SUTCLIFFE.

> He prayeth best who loveth best
> All things both great and small:
> For the dear God who loveth us,
> He made and loveth all.
>   COLERIDGE.

Prayer is the chief thing that man may present to God.   HERMES.

Prayer purifies; it is a self-preached sermon.
    RICHTER.

Prayer is the wing wherewith the soul flies to heaven, and meditation the eye wherewith we see God.   AMBROSE.

"When Pride leads the van,
Beggary brings up the rear."

Because you flourish in worldly affairs,
Don't be haughty and put on airs,
With insolent pride of station!
Don't be proud and turn up your nose
At poorer people in plainer clo'es,
But learn for the sake of your soul's repose
That wealth's a bubble that comes and goes,
And that all proud flesh, wherever it grows,
Is subject to irritation.   J. G. SAXE.

Pride (of all others the most dangerous fault)
Proceeds from want of sense or want of thought.
ROSCOMMON.

Pride is as loud a beggar as Want, and a
great deal more saucy. When you have bought
one fine thing, you must buy ten more, that
your appearance may be all of a piece; but it is
easier to suppress the first desire than to satisfy
all that follow it.   FRANKLIN.

PROCRASTINATION.

Procrastination is the thief of time.
YOUNG.

Delay leads impotent and snail-paced beggary.

PROCRASTINATION.

Be wise to-day; 'tis madness to defer.

YOUNG.

Omission to do what is necessary seals a commission to a blank of danger.

SHAKESPEARE.

By the street of " By and By,"
We arrive at the house of " Never."

Old Proverb.

That we would do,
We should do when we would, for this world changes.

SHAKESPEARE.

Unhappy he who does his work adjourn,
And to to-morrow would the search delay.
His lazy morrow will be like to-day.

DRYDEN.

Yesterday was once to-morrow.   PERSIUS.

It will not always be summer.   HESIOD.

Whatever things injure your Eye, you are anxious to remove ; but things which affect your Mind you defer.

HORACE.

Never defer that till to-morrow which you can do to-day.

BLUDGELL.

" One to-day is worth two to-morrows."

Oh! thou who mournest on thy way,
  With longings for the close of day,
He walks with thee, that angel kind,
  And gently whispers, " Be resigned:
Bear up, bear on, the end shall tell
  The dear Lord ordereth all things well!"
                                J. G. WHITTIER.

We must learn to suffer what we cannot evade.
                                MONTAIGNE.

      Things without remedy,
Should be without regard? what's done is done.
                                SHAKESPEARE.

REVENGE.

A feeling of revenge is not worth much, that
you should care to keep it.   GEORGE ELIOT.

The indulgence of revenge tends to make
men more savage and cruel.   LORD KAMES.

Hath any wronged thee? be bravely revenged;
sleight it and the work's begun; forgive it, 'tis
finisht: he is below himself that is not above an
injury.   QUARLES.

A man that studieth revenge keepeth his own
wounds green, which otherwise would heal and
do well.   LORD BACON.

Insist on yourself, never imitate.

R. W. EMERSON.

He who reigns within himself, and rules passions, desires and fears, is more than a king.

MILTON.

How many homes are embittered by fretfulness or jealousy, how many illnesses aggravated by peevishness or discontent, for want of knowing how to commence the difficult task of self-control.　　　　*Household Words.*

SELFISHNESS.

Self-love, my liege, is not so vile a sin as self-neglecting.　　　　SHAKESPEARE.

Selfishness is that detestable. vice which no one will forgive in others, and no one is without in himself.　　　　H. W. BEECHER.

Selfishness : a vice utterly at variance with the happiness of him who harbors it, and as such, condemned by self-love.

SIR J. MACKINTOSH.

Have a care how you keep company with those that, when they find themselves upon a pinch, will leave their friends in the lurch.

L'ESTRANGE.

There never did and never will exist anything permanently noble and excellent in a character which was a stranger to the exercise of resolute self-denial.   SCOTT.

Self-denial is a kind of holy association with God; and by making you his partner, interests you in all his happiness.   BOYLE.

The more a man denies himself, the more he shall obtain from God.   HORACE.

A good man not only forbears those gratifications which are forbidden by reason and religion, but even restrains himself in unforbidden instances.   ATTERBURY.

SERVING GOD.

The Lord our God will we serve and his voice will we obey.   *Bible.*

> And ye shall succor men;
>   'Tis nobleness to serve;
> Help them who cannot help again:
>   Beware from right to swerve.
>   EMERSON.

They also serve who only stand and wait.
              MILTON.

I couldn't live in peace if I put the shadow of a wilful sin between myself and God.

GEORGE ELIOT.

Sin is never at a stay; if we do not retreat from it, we shall advance in it; and the further on we go, the more we have to come back.

BARON.

He that falls into sin is a man; that grieves over it, may be a saint; that boasteth of it is a devil.

FULLER.

Man-like it is to fall in sin,
    Fiend-like it is to dwell therein,
Christ-like it is o'er sin to grieve,
    God-like it is all sin to leave.

LONGFELLOW.

SONS.

A wise son maketh a glad father: but a foolish son is the heaviness of his mother.

A wise son heareth his father's instructions.

Even a child is known by his doings, whether his work be pure, and whether it be right.

Bible.

72

If a boy is not trained to endure and to bear trouble, he will grow up a girl; and a boy that is a girl has all a girl's weakness without any of her regal qualities. A woman made out of a woman is God's noblest work; a woman made out of a man is his meanest.

H. W. BEECHER.

STRENGTH.

As the Sandwich Islander believes that the strength and valor of the enemy he kills passes into himself, so we gain the strength of the temptation we resist. R. W. EMERSON.

What is strength, without a double share
Of wisdom? Vast, unwieldy, burdensome;
Proudly secure, yet liable to fall
By weakest subtleties; not made to rule,
But to subserve where wisdom bears command.

MILTON.

Strength for to-day is all that we need,
  As there never will be a to-morrow,
For to-morrow will prove but another to-day
  With its measure of joy and of sorrow.

BUCKHAM.

73

TIME.

Life is not to be bought with heaps of gold ;
Not all Apollo's Pythian treasures hold,
Or Troy once held in peace and pride of sway,
Can bribe the poor possession of a day.

HOMER.

" Time is the present hour, the past has fled ;
Live ! live to-day ! to-morrow never yet
On any human being rose or set."

Dost thou love life ? Then waste not time,
for time is the stuff that life is made of.

FRANKLIN.

Time is painted with a lock before and bald
behind, signifying thereby that we must take
time by the forelock, for when it is once passed,
there is no recalling it.   DEAN SWIFT.

Time is the only gift in which God has stinted
us, for He never intrusts us with a second moment until He has taken away the first, and never
leaves us certain of the third.

RUTHERFORD.

Time is the warp of life, said he. Oh tell
The young, the fair, the gay, to weave it well.

MARSDEN.

74

TIME.

Hours are golden links, God's token
Reaching heaven, but one by one,
Take them, lest the chain be broken
Ere the pilgrimage be done.

A. A. PROCTER.

No man can be provident of his time that is not provident in the choice of his company.

DR. JOHNSON.

Time can be utilized best by those who are well, and every girl should mean to be well, cheery, and strong if she can. To this end she should neglect nothing which God puts within her reach for the preservation of health, animation and vigor.

We have each the same number of hours in every day, and the queen in her palace has just as many as, and no more than, the little maiden who carries her father's dinner to the mill. In this one particular God has treated us all precisely alike.

Time is ours, not to be wasted, not to be spent in luxurious ease, and not to be lost in idle fretting. It is ours to be improved.

MARGARET E. SANGSTER.

"How gentle God's commands!
How kind his precepts are!
Come cast your burden on the Lord
And trust his constant care."

As thy days, so shall thy strength be.

Bible.

All I have seen teaches me to trust the Creator for all I have not seen.

R. W. EMERSON.

TRUTH.

I would have a woman as true as Death. At the first real lie which works from the heart outward, she should be tenderly chloroformed into a better world, where she can have an angel for a governess, and feed on strange fruits which will make her over again, even to her bones and marrow.

Leave what you've done for what you have to
    do,
Don't be consistent, but be simply true.

O. W. HOLMES.

"It is in the determination to obey the truth, and to follow wherever she may lead, that the genuine love of truth consists."

TRUTH.

"Truth is honest, truth is sure;
Truth is strong and must endure;
Falsehood lasts a single day,
Then it vanishes away."

The greatest friend of Truth is Time, her greatest enemy is Prejudice, and her constant companion is Humility.　　　COLTON.

Defeat is the school in which Truth always grows strong.　　　H. W. BEECHER.

In fact there's nothing that keeps its youth
So far as I know, but a tree and truth.
　　　　　O. W. HOLMES.

Be always precisely true in whatever thou relatest of thy own knowledge; that thou mayst give an undoubted and settled reputation for veracity.　　　THOMAS FULLER.

"The truth of truths is love."

Shuffling may serve for a time, but truth will most certainly carry it at the long run.
　　　　　L'ESTRANGE.

" 'Tis not the many oaths that make the truth,
But the plain vow that is vowed true."

"The nimble lie
Is like the second-hand upon a clock.
We see it fly; while the hour-hand of truth
Seems to stand still, and yet it moves unseen
And wins at last, for the clock will not strike
Till it has reached the goal."

USE OF TIME.

Six hours in sleep, in law's grave study six,
Four spend in prayer — the rest on nature fix.

SIR EDW. COKE.

Seven hours to law, to soothing slumber seven,
Ten to the world allot, and all to heaven.

SIR WM. JONES.

Eight hours and a half to school allot,
  To soothing slumber nine,
The rest to home and friends devote,
  Excepting three — to dine.

A. L. COWAN.

Eight hours to study give, to dreamland nine,
Three more to deeds of love, and two to dine,
Two to amusement say, but all to God divine.

LOUISE ROUSSEL.

Vice is a monster of such hideous mien
That to be hated needs but to be seen;
But seen too oft, familiar with her face,
We first endure, then pity, then embrace.

POPE.

Vice incapacitates a man from all public duty; it withers the powers of his understanding, and makes his mind paralytic. BURKE.

As a stick, when once it is dry and stiff, you may break it, but you can never bend it into a straighter posture, so doth the man become incorrigible who is settled and stiffened in vice.

BARROW.

VIRTUE.

The four cardinal virtues are prudence, fortitude, temperance and patience. PALEY.

All virtue lies in a power of denying our own desires where reason does not authorize them.

LOCKE.

All true virtues are to honor true religion as their parent, and all well-ordered commonwealths to love her as their chief stay.

HOOKER.

If thou do ill, the joy fades not the pains ;
If well, the pain doth fade, the joy remains.
GEORGE ELIOT.

That's what I always say, if you wish a thing to
    be well done
You must do it yourself; you must not leave it
    to others.   LONGFELLOW.

    Do not look for wrong and evil,
      You will find them if you do ;
    As you measure for your neighbor,
      He will measure back for you.
ALICE CARY.

WISDOM.

Wisdom is oft times nearer when we stoop
than when we soar.   WORDSWORTH.

He is the wisest man who is most susceptible
of alteration.   BACON.

What doth better become wisdom than to dis-
cern what is worthy the living?
SIR PHILIP SIDNEY.

Never be ashamed to own you were in the
wrong, which is but saying you are wiser to-day
than yesterday.   O. W. HOLMES.

WOMEN.

These poor silly women-things — they've not the sense to know it's no use denying what's proved. '

Half the sorrows of women would be averted if they could repress the speech they know to be useless — nay, the speech they have resolved not to utter.

A woman, let her be as good as she may, has got to put up with the life her husband makes for her.   GEORGE ELIOT.

O, what is woman! what her smile,
    Her lips of love, her eyes of light!
What is she, if her lips revile
    The lowly Jesus?   Love may write
His name above her marble brow,
    May linger in her curls of jet,
The light spring flowers may scarcely bow
    Beneath her feet — and yet — and yet —
Without that meeker grace, she'd be —
    A lighter thing than vanity.
                                   N. P. WILLIS.
                        (*From an unpublished poem.*)

WORDS.

Good words make friends; bad words make enemies. SIR MATTHEW HALE.

"For words like nature — half reveal
And half conceal the soul within."

"Thought is deeper than all speech;
Feeling deeper than all thought."

Give not thy tongue too great a liberty lest it take thee prisoner. QUARLES.

He that hath a perverse tongue falleth into mischief.

A soft answer turneth away wrath; but grievous words stir up anger.

A wholesome tongue is a tree of life, but perverseness therein is a breach in the spirit.
Bible.

The right word is always a power, and communicates its definiteness to our action.
GEORGE ELIOT.

But words are things and a small drop of ink,
Falling like dew upon a thought, produces
That which makes thousands, perhaps millions
think. BYRON.

WORDS.

" If you've anything to say
True and needed, yea or nay,
Say it."

There is only one thing that is more terrible than to say a mean thing, and that is to do one.

SIR WM. HARCOURT.

Learn to hold thy tongue. Five words cost Zacharias forty weeks' silence.

THOMAS FULLER.

An unlucky word once escaped from us, cannot be brought back with a coach and six.

Chinese Proverb.

A helping word to one in trouble is often like a switch on a railroad track — but one inch between wreck and smooth-rolling prosperity.

H. W. BEECHER.

What you keep by you, you may change and mend; but words once spoke can never be recalled.

ROSCOMMON.

A word fitly spoken is like apples of gold in pictures of silver.

Bible.

Speak well of the absent whenever you have a suitable opportunity.

SIR MATTHEW HALE.

WORK.

Those who toil bravely are strongest;
  The humble and poor become great,
And so from these brown-handed children
  Shall grow mighty rulers of state.
M. H. KROUT.

"It is the cheery worker that succeeds. No one can do his best, or even do well, in the midst of worry or nagging. Wherefore if you work, work as cheerily as you can. If you do not work, do not put even a straw in the way of others."

Brave hearts, true hearts, no duty shirk;
Labor, "The Salt of Life is Work."
Harper's Weekly.

Blessed is he who has found his work; let him ask no other blessedness.
THOMAS CARLYLE.

God never accepts a good inclination instead of a good action, where that action may be done; nay, so much the contrary, that if a good inclination be not seconded by a good action, the want of that action is made so much the more criminal and inexcusable. SOUTH.

WORK.

He does the best work in this moping, croaking age, whose cheerful face gives the benediction of a happy heart, wherever a heavy step is treading along just behind him.

CHAS. S. ROBINSON.

All service is the same with God —
With God, whose puppets, best and worst,
Are we: there is no last nor first.

ROBERT BROWNING.

Labor is man's great function.   He is nothing, he can be nothing, he can achieve nothing, he can fulfill nothing without labor.

ORVILLE DEWEY.

Each morning sees some task begun,
    Each evening sees it close ;
Something attempted, something done,
    Has earned a night's repose.

LONGFELLOW.

Work for some good, be it ever so slowly !
Cherish some flower, be it ever so lowly.
Labor ! all labor is noble and holy ;
Let thy great deed be thy prayer to thy God.

F. S. OSGOOD.

WORK — WRONG-DOING.

"Do not then stand idly waiting
  For some greater work to do;
Fortune is a lazy goddess,
  She will never come to you.
Go and toil in any vineyard;
  Do not fear to do or dare;
If you want a field of labor,
  You can find it anywhere."

"Work sows the seed;
Even the *rock* may yield its flower —
No lot so hard but human power,
  Exerted to one end and aim,
  May conquer fate, and capture fame!
    Press on!"

  Free men freely work:
Whoever fears God, fears to sit at ease.

MRS. BROWNING.

WRONG-DOING.

You cannot do wrong without suffering wrong.

R. W. EMERSON.

Nothing can work me damage except myself;
the harm that I sustain I carry about with me,
and never am a real sufferer but by my own
fault. ST. BERNARD.

86

MISCELLANEOUS.

Cause and effect are two sides of one fact.

Nature never rhymes her children, nor makes two men alike.

We aim above the mark, to hit the mark.

R. W. EMERSON.

There is no substitute for thorough-going, ardent and sincere earnestness.

CHARLES DICKENS.

The talent of success is nothing more than doing what you can do well, and doing well whatever you do, without a thought of fame.

LONGFELLOW.

He who seduously attends, pointedly asks, calmly speaks, coolly answers, and ceases when he has no more to say, is in possession of some of the best requisites of man.

LAVATER.

Silently sat the artist alone,
  Carving a Christ from the ivory bone ;
Little by little, with toil and pain
  He won his way through the sightless grain,
That held and yet hid the thing he sought,
  Till the work stood up a growing thought.

BOKER.

MISCELLANEOUS.

There's a divinity that shapes our ends,
Rough-hew them as we will.

SHAKESPEARE.

Dispatch is the soul of business.

CHESTERFIELD.

Conscience doth make cowards of us all.

SHAKESPEARE.

You question the justice which governs man's
    breast,
And say that the search for true friendship is
    vain;
But remember, this world, though it be not the
    best,
Is the next to the best we shall ever attain.

CHARLES SWAIN.

Take the Sunday with you through the week,
And with it sweeten all the other days.

LONGFELLOW.

Endeavor to be first in thy calling, whatever
it be; neither let any one go before thee in
well-doing; nevertheless do not envy the merits
of another, but improve thine own talents.

DODSLEY.

In this world, it is not what we take up, but what we give up, that makes us rich.

H. W. BEECHER.

The first condition of human goodness is something to love, the second, something to reverence. GEORGE ELIOT.

" In private watch your thoughts ; in your family watch your temper ; in society watch your tongue."

Yea ; find thou always time to say some earnest word
Between the idle talk, lest with thee henceforth,
Night and day, regret should walk.

COVENTRY PATMORE.

Learn as if you were to live forever ; live as if you were to die to-morrow.

ANSALUS DE INSULIS.

A good name is rather to be chosen than great riches. *Bible.*

God helps those that help themselves.

FRANKLIN.

Put your trust in God, my boys, and keep your powder dry. OLIVER CROMWELL.

MISCELLANEOUS.

Be sure you're right and then go ahead.

DAVY CROCKETT.

"A well-spent day prepares us for sweet repose."

I hold it truth, with him who sings
To one clear harp in divers tones,
That men may rise on stepping-stones
Of their dead selves to higher things.

TENNYSON.

And when you stick on conversation's burs,
Don't strew your pathway with those dreadful urs.

O. W. HOLMES.

No two things differ more than hurry and dispatch. Hurry is the mark of a weak mind, dispatch of a strong one.

COLTON.

Every one is the son of his own works.

CERVANTES.

Once a day, especially in the early years of life and study, call yourselves to an account — what new ideas, what new proposition or truth you have gained.

DR. ISAAC WATTS.

New actions are the only apologies and explanations of old ones which the noble can bear to offer or to receive.

R. W. EMERSON.

90

Difficulties are God's errands. And when we are sent upon them we should esteem it a proof of God's confidence — as a compliment from God.   H. W. BEECHER.

How beautiful the long mild twilight, which, like a silver clasp, unites to-day with yesterday.

The heart hath its own memory, like the mind,
And in it are enshrined
The precious keepsakes, into which are wrought
The giver's loving thought.   LONGFELLOW.

It behooves the high for their own sakes to do things worthily.   BEN JONSON.

Speak out in acts ; the time for words has passed, and deeds alone remain.
     J. G. WHITTIER.

The best fire doesna flare up the soonest.

We are led on, like little children, by a way that we know not.   GEORGE ELIOT.

Night wrapped her sable mantle round, and pinned it with a star.   LOUIS GAYLORD CLARK.

Silently, one by one, in the infinite meadows of
　　heaven,
Blossom the lovely stars, the forget-me-nots of
　　the angels.　　　　　　　LONGFELLOW.

Prove all things ; hold fast that which is good.

Let not the sun go down upon your wrath.

These six things doth the Lord hate, yea,
seven are an abomination to him :
A proud look, a lying tongue, and hands that
shed innocent blood,
A heart that deviseth wicked imaginations,
feet that be swift in running to mischief,
A false witness that speaketh lies, and he
that soweth discord among brethren.

Pure religion and undefiled before God and
the Father is this, To visit the fatherless and
widows in their affliction, and to keep himself
unspotted from the world.　　　　　*Bible.*

From envy, hatred, and malice, and all un-
charitableness, good Lord, deliver us.
　　　　　　　Book of Common Prayer.

"Mirth should be the embroidery of conversation, not the web, and wit the ornament of mind, not the furniture."

The real price of everything, what everything really costs to the man who wants to acquire it, is the toil and trouble of acquiring it.

ADAM SMITH.

Dear to us are those who love us; the swift moments we spend with them are a compensation for a great deal of misery: they enlarge our life — but dearer are they who reject us as unworthy, for they add another life; they build a heaven before us whereof we had not dreamed, and thereby supply to us new powers out of the recesses of the spirit, and urge us to new and unattempted performances.   R. W. EMERSON.

A noble mind disdains not to repent.

HOMER.

A thought often makes us hotter than a fire.

As turning the logs will make a dull fire burn, so change of studies a dull brain.

LONGFELLOW.

Every kernel has its shell,
Every chime its harshest bell,
Every face its weariest look,
Every shelf its emptiest book,
Every field its leanest sheaf,
Every book its dullest leaf,
Every leaf its weakest line, —
Shall it not be so with mine ?
Best for worst shall make amends,
Find us, keep us, leave us friends
Till perchance we meet again,
Benedicite — Amen.   O. W. HOLMES.

Christian life consists in faith and charity.
MARTIN LUTHER.

Never ask a question if you can help it; and
never let a thing go unknown for the lack of
asking a question, if you can't help it.
H. W. BEECHER.

He who does the utmost that he can, always
does more than he alone could have accom-
plished; for God is working with him and makes
his little mighty.   W. M. TAYLOR.

The great lesson of travel is toleration.
CURTIS.

94

Letters, such as are written from wise men, are of all the words of men, in my judgment, the best.   LORD BACON.

Never risk a joke even the least offensive in its nature, and the most common, with a person who is not well-bred and possessed of sense to comprehend it.   LA BRUYÈRE.

A home is never perfectly furnished for enjoyment, unless there is a child in it, rising three years old, and a kitten rising three weeks.
                                            SOUTHEY.

It is better to inspire the heart with a noble sentiment than to teach the mind a truth of science.   EDWARD BURKE.

All nature is but art unknown to thee;
All chance, direction which thou canst not see;
All discord, harmony not understood;
All partial evil, universal good;
And spite of pride, in erring reason's spite,
One truth is clear: *Whatever is, is right.*
                                            POPE.

The reward of one duty is the power to fulfill another — so said Ben Azar.   GEORGE ELIOT.

MISCELLANEOUS.

A man must not choose his neighbor: he must take the neighbor that God sends him.
GEORGE MACDONALD.

" A godly life is the only evidence of a changed heart."

Neither days nor lives can be made holy by doing nothing in them.
RUSKIN.

One likes a "beyond" everywhere.
GEORGE ELIOT.

Honor makes a great part of the reward of all honorable professions.
ADAM SMITH.

In a sense, what a man wants he can have. The desire of his soul is the prophecy of his fate.
O. W. HOLMES, JR.

Without confidence in one's self very little headway is made in this world.
J. G. HOLLAND.

Learning means being taught to think by easy steps.

Thought is a pleasure and a power.
THRING.

MISCELLANEOUS.

Highest aim and true endeavor,
  Earnest work with patient might;
Hoping, trusting, singing ever;
  Battling bravely for the right;

Loving God, all men forgiving,
  Helping weaker feet to stand—
These will make a life worth living,
  Make it noble, make it grand.
EMMA C. DOWD.

"The universe is not quite perfect without *my* work well done."

Young folks are sometimes very cunning in finding out contrivances to cheat themselves.
SHERLOCK.

"When you've nothing to say, say it."

"Nothing not good is wanted."

We can't talk unless we know what we ought to say, what we mean to say, what we do say, and to whom we say it.   H. CLAY TRUMBULL.

The world continues to exist only by the breath of the children of the schools.
Talmud.

Conscience is the whisper of God.
J. R. MILLER.

97

At sermon and at prayers men may sleep and wander, but when one is asked a question he must disclose what he is.   GEORGE HERBERT.

Oh! be it mine with deed or song,
To kindle some life to purpose strong;
To light some lamp on the shore of time,
That shall shine forever with beam sublime!
                              JAMES BUCKHAM.

Do not consider that for your interest, which makes you break your word, or inclines you to any practice which will not bear the light, or look the world in the face.   ANTONINUS.

Canst thou bind the sweet influences of the Pleiades or loose the bands of Orion? Canst thou bring forth Mazzaroth in his season? or canst thou bind Arcturus and his sons?
                                        Bible.

The rain has spoiled the farmer's day,
Shall sorrow put my books away?
Thereby are two days lost:
Nature shall mind her own affairs,
I will attend my proper cares
In rain, or sun, or frost.   R. .W EMERSON.

Do what we can, summer will have its flies;
if we walk in the woods, we must feel mosqui-
toes; if we go a-fishing, we must expect a wet
coat.   R. W. EMERSON.

> Evil swells the debt to pay,
> Good delivers and acquits;
> Shun evil, follow good; hold sway
> Over thyself.   This is the way.
> > EDWIN ARNOLD.

Seize the moment of excited curiosity on any
subject, to solve your doubts; for if you let it
pass, the desire may never return, and you may
remain in ignorance.   Therefore seize the moment of excited curiosity and look it up!
                                    WIRT.

> Cast all your cares on God: that anchor holds—
> Is he not yonder in the uttermost
> Parts of the morning? if I flee to these
> Can I go from Him? and the sea is His,
> The sea is His: He made it.
> > TENNYSON.

Evil reports often originate by spontaneous
combustion in the protoplasm of total depravity.
                            HOMER B. SPRAGUE.

Surely there is something in the unruffled calm of nature that overawes our little anxieties and doubts: the sight of the deep blue sky and the clustering stars above, seem to impart a quiet to the mind. JONATHAN EDWARDS.

> Ah ! let us hope that to our praise
> Good God not only reckons
> The moments when we tread his ways,
> But when the spirit beckons, —
> That some slight good is also wrought
> Beyond self-satisfaction,
> When we are simply good in thought,
> Howe'er we fail in action.
>   J. R. LOWELL.

We are all building a soul house for eternity; yet with what different architecture, and what various care. H. W. BEECHER.

Therefore to him that knoweth to do good, and doeth it not, to him it is sin. *Bible.*

When we have practiced good actions awhile they become easy; and when they are easy, we begin to take pleasure in them; and when they · please us, we do them frequently; and by frequency of acts, they grow into a habit.

MISCELLANEOUS.

A poem, — magical words and thoughts,
　　Like a flower of wondrous bloom,
Its fancies, the color catching the light,
　　Its deeper sense, the perfume.
　　　　　　　　　PALMER D. HATCH.

A large part of my religion consists in trying
all the while not to be as mean as I know
how.　　　　　　PETROLEUM V. NASEBY.

If we are left in the world another year, it is
that we may do our share of the world's work.
　　　　　　　　　ROBT. McKENZIE.

**THIS BOOK IS DUE ON THE LAST DATE
STAMPED BELOW**

AN INITIAL FINE OF 25 CENTS
WILL BE ASSESSED FOR FAILURE TO RETURN
THIS BOOK ON THE DATE DUE. THE PENALTY
WILL INCREASE TO 50 CENTS ON THE FOURTH
DAY AND TO $1.00 ON THE SEVENTH DAY
OVERDUE.

FEB 26 1941 M

21 Jan '59 KY

REC'D LD

JAN 16 1959

CPSIA information can be obtained
at www.ICGtesting.com
Printed in the USA
BVHW06*1108091018
529683BV00012B/204/P